DATE			

Tukama Tootles the Flute

A TALE FROM THE ANTILLES

retold by **Phillis Gershator**

paintings by **Synthia Saint James**

Orchard Books **New York**

Orchard Books, 95 Madison Avenue, New York, NY 10016

Manufactured in the United States of America. Printed by Barton Press, Inc.
Bound by Horowitz/Rae. Book design by Mina Greenstein.
The text of this book is set in 16 point Trajanus Bold. The illustrations are oil paintings reproduced in full color. 10 9 8 7 6 5 4 3 2 1

Library of Congress Cataloging-in-Publication Data
Gershator, Phillis. Tukama tootles the flute : a tale from the Antilles / retold by Phillis Gershator ; paintings by Synthia Saint James.
p. cm. "A Richard Jackson book"—Half t.p.
Summary: When Tukama is captured by a two-headed giant and held prisoner by the giant's wife, he uses his flute to escape.
ISBN 0-531-06811-0. ISBN 0-531-08661-5 (lib. bdg.)
[1. Folklore—Virgin Islands of the United States. 2. Giants—Folklore.] I. Saint James, Synthia, ill. II. Title PZ8.1G353Tu 1994 398.21—dc20 [E] 93-2253

To all the flute tootlers in my family

—P.G.

To my godchild, Jessica

—S.S.J.

ONCE UPON A TIME, on a little rocky island in the Caribbean Sea, there lived a boy and his grandmother. This boy, Tukama, was very wild. Instead of helping his grandmother carry the coal, fetch water, and dig up potatoes in the yard, he'd run off and play. He'd stay away all day, until it was dark outside.

He ran along the beach nibbling on sea grapes. Then he wandered around the hills, picking mango and papaya. Then he climbed up and down the dangerous rocks on the north shore and whiled away the time tootling his flute.

When he got home, his worried grandmother said,
"Where you been, boy? It late! Don't you know a
two-headed giant runnin' about here, lookin' for wild
children to eat?"

"Oh, Grandma," he said back, "you makin' joke!"

"Me son! Why do you think all those children *gone*
that climbed around the rocks? It wasn't the sea took
'em. It was the two-headed giant." Grandma even sucked
her teeth, she was so upset with Tukama.

But he didn't heed Grandma's words. He ran off and did as he pleased.

One day, Tukama went running up to a high place where the land overlooked the sea. The rocky cliffs were steep there, and the waves churned and frothed in the whirlpools below. He climbed down the rocks and stood in the spray of the crashing waves. He was having so much fun he didn't notice the sun going down. When he finally climbed back up the rocks, it was dark. He took out his flute and tootled on it to keep himself company in the night.

"All right, boy. Get on my big toe, and play that song for me again."

So Tukama stood on the giant's big toe and tootled and sang,

"Tanto, tanto, tango,
Guavaberry, mango,
Bombwiti, bombwiti,
Bimbala, bango."

"All right, boy. Jump on my knee. I can't hear that song well enough."

Tukama jumped on the giant's knee and tootled and sang,

"*Tanto, tanto, tango,*
Guavaberry, mango,
Bombwiti, bombwiti,
Bimbala, bango."

"All right, boy. Climb up on
my chest, and play that
song louder."
Tukama climbed up on the
giant's chest and tootled
and sang,

"Tanto, tanto, tango,
Guavaberry, mango,
Bombwiti, bombwiti,
Bimbala, bango."

"All right, boy. Stand here on my nose and play that song one more time."

"Which nose?" Tukama asked.

"This one, boy!" But when the giant took a breath and smelled a human child's scent up close, he got hungry. He plucked Tukama off his nose and stuffed him in a bag.

"That's enough singin' for today," the giant said. "I'll take this boy home and fatten him up for food."

With three big giant steps, he climbed down the rocks into his cave.

He gave his wife the bag and said, "I got a nice boy in here. Want you to fatten him up for me."

"All right," she said, and she threw some fried johnnycakes into the bag. She knew human children liked johnnycakes.

As for the giants, they ate whole prickly pears, prickles and all, and whole raw fish, bones and all, and sprinkled them both with poisonous red jumbie beads. If human beings ate unpeeled prickly pears, the prickles would stick like pins and needles in their lips. If human beings ate whole raw fish, the bones would stick like thorns in their throats. And if human beings ate poisonous red jumbie beads, they would die! But two-headed giants eat those things, and what happens? Nothing. They just rub their bellies and say, *"Yum, yum, yum!"*

When the giant went out in the morning to catch fish and collect prickly pears and jumbie beads, he told his wife, "Give that boy a lot of johnnycake today. Fatten him up good, and we'll eat him for supper."

As soon as the giant left,
Tukama tootled his flute and sang,

"Tanto, tanto, taya,
Tamarind, papaya,
Mama lama, cuma lama,
Mama lama laya."

The giant's wife said, "Little boy, little boy, play that song again!"

Tukama said, "Could you open the bag a wee bit, so I can get some air?"

"All right, little boy." And she let Tukama come out of the bag up to his nose.

He tootled and sang,

"Tanto, tanto, taya,
Tamarind, papaya,
Mama lama, cuma lama,
Mama lama laya."

"Little boy, little boy, play that song again!"
Tukama said, "If you open the bag a wee bit and let my
hands come out, I can make you dance on your toes."
She opened the bag enough for Tukama's hands to come out.

He tootled and sang,

"*Tanto, tanto, taya,*
Tamarind, papaya,
Mama lama, cuma lama,
Mama lama laya,"

until she danced on her toes.

When he stopped, she cried, "Little boy, little boy, play that song again!"

Tukama answered, "If you let me come out of the bag, I can make you dance on your head."

So she let him out of the bag. And while he was tootling and singing,

"*Tanto, tanto, taya,*
Tamarind, papaya,
Mama lama, cuma lama,
Mama lama laya,"

she danced on her head, and he kept backing away and backing away, and then — away he ran!

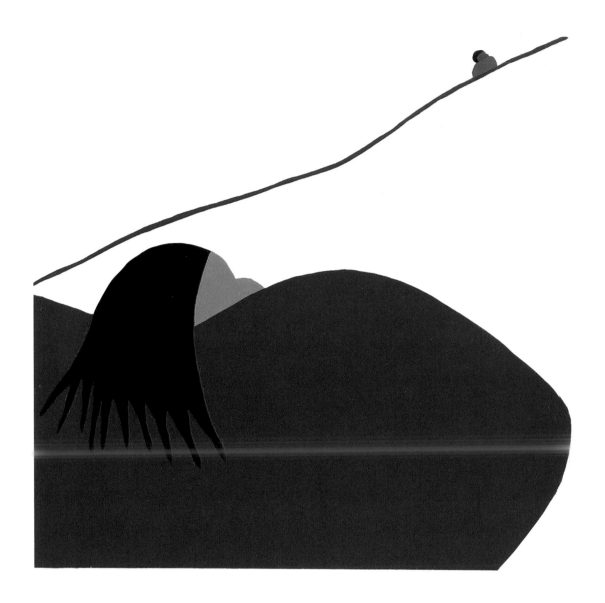

By the time she righted herself, Tukama was already halfway up the rocks. She ran behind him crying, "Little boy, little boy, come back, come back! Play that song again!"

But Tukama did not go back. In fact, he stayed away
from the rocks from then on. And when he played that song
again, he played it for his grandmother after he had helped
to carry the coal, fetch water, and dig up potatoes in the yard.

"*Tanto, tanto, taya,*
Tamarind, papaya,
Mama lama, cuma lama,
Mama lama laya."

AUTHOR'S NOTE

This retelling freely adapts story seven from St. Thomas in Elsie Clews Parsons's *Folk-Lore of the Antilles, French and English, Part II* (New York: American Folk-Lore Society, 1936). The songs are a combination of nonsense words from children's chants and the song in the original story,

> *Tanto, tanto,*
> *Oh, the woman bury the guava berry,*
> *Tanto, tanto, tanto.*

When I situated the giants' den beneath a rocky cliff, I was thinking of Magen's Point on St. Thomas, a scenic and dangerous spot where whirlpools and waves have claimed the lives of many, despite cautionary warnings. Fishermen fish off the rocks, and cactus and jumbie beads grow there, which accounts for the giants' daily diet.

As for jumbie beads, the all-red ones (*Adenathear pavonia*) are not poisonous, according to Doris Jadan in her book *A Guide to the Natural History of St. John*. According to a fact sheet from the University of the Virgin Islands, the poisonous ones, red with a black dot, or "eye," are *Abrus precatorius. Abrus* is native to India. It was used for money and jewelry and brought to Africa along trade routes. (I have seen the seeds adorning old African statues.) It's likely both seeds were imported to the Caribbean from West Africa. In St. Croix, one name for jumbie beads is *ko-kre-ko,* surely African in origin.

Local johnnycake is round, deep-fried bread about an inch thick and four or five inches in diameter.